NATIONAL PARKS
Journal

This Journal Belongs To

NAME	
PHONE	
EMAIL	
ADDRESS	
NOTES	

NATIONAL PARKS *Journal*

DATE(S) | VISITED
☐ SPRING ☐ SUMMER ☐ FALL ☐ WINTER

MY FAVORITE MOMENT

WHO I WENT WITH

LODING

WEATHER

FEE(S)	
☐ FEE(S)	☐ FREE

SIGHTS

WILDLIFE

POPULAR ATTRACTIONS I VISITED	
☐	☐
☐	☐
☐	☐

OVERALL EXPERIENCE

NATIONAL PARKS *Journal*

DATE(S) | VISITED

☐ SPRING ☐ SUMMER ☐ FALL ☐ WINTER

MY FAVORITE MOMENT

WHO I WENT WITH

LODING

WEATHER

FEE(S)

☐ FEE(S) ☐ FREE

SIGHTS

WILDLIFE

POPULAR ATTRACTIONS I VISITED

☐ ☐
☐ ☐
☐ ☐

OVERALL EXPERIENCE

NATIONAL PARKS *Journal*

DATE(S) | VISITED

☐ SPRING ☐ SUMMER ☐ FALL ☐ WINTER

MY FAVORITE MOMENT

WHO I WENT WITH

LODING

WEATHER

FEE(S)

☐ FEE(S) ☐ FREE

SIGHTS

WILDLIFE

POPULAR ATTRACTIONS I VISITED

☐	☐
☐	☐
☐	☐

OVERALL EXPERIENCE

NATIONAL PARKS *Journal*

DATE(S) | VISITED
☐ SPRING ☐ SUMMER ☐ FALL ☐ WINTER

WHO I WENT WITH

LODING

MY FAVORITE MOMENT

WEATHER

FEE(S)
☐ FEE(S) ☐ FREE

SIGHTS

WILDLIFE

POPULAR ATTRACTIONS I VISITED	
☐	☐
☐	☐
☐	☐

OVERALL EXPERIENCE

NATIONAL PARKS *Journal*

DATE(S) | VISITED

☐ SPRING ☐ SUMMER ☐ FALL ☐ WINTER

MY FAVORITE MOMENT

WHO I WENT WITH

LODING

WEATHER

FEE(S)

☐ FEE(S) ☐ FREE

SIGHTS

WILDLIFE

POPULAR ATTRACTIONS I VISITED

☐	☐
☐	☐
☐	☐

OVERALL EXPERIENCE

NATIONAL PARKS *Journal*

DATE(S) | VISITED
☐ SPRING ☐ SUMMER ☐ FALL ☐ WINTER

MY FAVORITE MOMENT

WHO I WENT WITH

LODING

WEATHER

FEE(S)	
☐ FEE(S)	☐ FREE

SIGHTS

WILDLIFE

POPULAR ATTRACTIONS I VISITED	
☐	☐
☐	☐
☐	☐

OVERALL EXPERIENCE

NATIONAL PARKS *Journal*

DATE(S) | VISITED

☐ SPRING ☐ SUMMER ☐ FALL ☐ WINTER

MY FAVORITE MOMENT

WHO I WENT WITH

LODING

WEATHER

FEE(S)

☐ FEE(S) ☐ FREE

SIGHTS

WILDLIFE

POPULAR ATTRACTIONS I VISITED

☐ ☐
☐ ☐
☐ ☐

OVERALL EXPERIENCE

NATIONAL PARKS *Journal*

DATE(S) | VISITED

☐ SPRING ☐ SUMMER ☐ FALL ☐ WINTER

MY FAVORITE MOMENT

WHO I WENT WITH

LODING

WEATHER

FEE(S)

☐ FEE(S) ☐ FREE

SIGHTS

WILDLIFE

POPULAR ATTRACTIONS I VISITED

☐ ☐
☐ ☐
☐ ☐

OVERALL EXPERIENCE

NATIONAL PARKS *Journal*

DATE(S) | VISITED
☐ SPRING ☐ SUMMER ☐ FALL ☐ WINTER

MY FAVORITE MOMENT

WHO I WENT WITH

LODING

WEATHER

FEE(S)	
☐ FEE(S)	☐ FREE

SIGHTS

WILDLIFE

POPULAR ATTRACTIONS I VISITED	
☐	☐
☐	☐
☐	☐

OVERALL EXPERIENCE

NATIONAL PARKS *Journal*

DATE(S) | VISITED
☐ SPRING ☐ SUMMER ☐ FALL ☐ WINTER

MY FAVORITE MOMENT

WHO I WENT WITH

LODING

WEATHER

FEE(S)
☐ FEE(S) ☐ FREE

SIGHTS

WILDLIFE

POPULAR ATTRACTIONS I VISITED	
☐	☐
☐	☐
☐	☐

OVERALL EXPERIENCE

NATIONAL PARKS *Journal*

DATE(S) | VISITED
☐ SPRING ☐ SUMMER ☐ FALL ☐ WINTER

MY FAVORITE MOMENT

WHO I WENT WITH

LODING

WEATHER

FEE(S)	
☐ FEE(S)	☐ FREE

SIGHTS

WILDLIFE

POPULAR ATTRACTIONS I VISITED	
☐	☐
☐	☐
☐	☐

OVERALL EXPERIENCE

NATIONAL PARKS *Journal*

DATE(S) | VISITED

☐ SPRING ☐ SUMMER ☐ FALL ☐ WINTER

MY FAVORITE MOMENT

WHO I WENT WITH

LODING

WEATHER

FEE(S)

☐ FEE(S) ☐ FREE

SIGHTS

WILDLIFE

POPULAR ATTRACTIONS I VISITED

☐	☐
☐	☐
☐	☐

OVERALL EXPERIENCE

NATIONAL PARKS *Journal*

DATE(S) | VISITED

☐ SPRING ☐ SUMMER ☐ FALL ☐ WINTER

MY FAVORITE MOMENT

WHO I WENT WITH

LODING

WEATHER

FEE(S)

☐ FEE(S) ☐ FREE

SIGHTS

WILDLIFE

POPULAR ATTRACTIONS I VISITED

☐	☐
☐	☐
☐	☐

OVERALL EXPERIENCE

NATIONAL PARKS *Journal*

DATE(S) | VISITED

☐ SPRING ☐ SUMMER ☐ FALL ☐ WINTER

MY FAVORITE MOMENT

WHO I WENT WITH

LODING

WEATHER

FEE(S)

☐ FEE(S) ☐ FREE

SIGHTS

WILDLIFE

POPULAR ATTRACTIONS I VISITED

☐	☐
☐	☐
☐	☐

OVERALL EXPERIENCE

NATIONAL PARKS *Journal*

DATE(S) | VISITED

☐ SPRING ☐ SUMMER ☐ FALL ☐ WINTER

MY FAVORITE MOMENT

WHO I WENT WITH

LODING

WEATHER

FEE(S)

☐ FEE(S) ☐ FREE

SIGHTS

WILDLIFE

POPULAR ATTRACTIONS I VISITED

☐	☐
☐	☐
☐	☐

OVERALL EXPERIENCE

NATIONAL PARKS *Journal*

DATE(S) | VISITED

☐ SPRING ☐ SUMMER ☐ FALL ☐ WINTER

MY FAVORITE MOMENT

WHO I WENT WITH

LODING

WEATHER

FEE(S)

☐ FEE(S) ☐ FREE

SIGHTS

WILDLIFE

POPULAR ATTRACTIONS I VISITED

☐	☐
☐	☐
☐	☐

OVERALL EXPERIENCE

NATIONAL PARKS *Journal*

DATE(S) | VISITED

☐ SPRING ☐ SUMMER ☐ FALL ☐ WINTER

MY FAVORITE MOMENT

WHO I WENT WITH

LODING

WEATHER

FEE(S)

☐ FEE(S) ☐ FREE

SIGHTS

WILDLIFE

POPULAR ATTRACTIONS I VISITED

☐	☐
☐	☐
☐	☐

OVERALL EXPERIENCE

NATIONAL PARKS *Journal*

DATE(S) | VISITED
☐ SPRING ☐ SUMMER ☐ FALL ☐ WINTER

WHO I WENT WITH

MY FAVORITE MOMENT

LODING

WEATHER

FEE(S)	
☐ FEE(S)	☐ FREE

SIGHTS

WILDLIFE

POPULAR ATTRACTIONS I VISITED	
☐	☐
☐	☐
☐	☐

OVERALL EXPERIENCE

NATIONAL PARKS *Journal*

DATE(S) | VISITED

☐ SPRING ☐ SUMMER ☐ FALL ☐ WINTER

MY FAVORITE MOMENT

WHO I WENT WITH

LODING

WEATHER

FEE(S)

☐ FEE(S) ☐ FREE

SIGHTS

WILDLIFE

POPULAR ATTRACTIONS I VISITED

☐	☐
☐	☐
☐	☐

OVERALL EXPERIENCE

NATIONAL PARKS *Journal*

DATE(S) | VISITED
☐ SPRING ☐ SUMMER ☐ FALL ☐ WINTER

MY FAVORITE MOMENT

WHO I WENT WITH

LODING

WEATHER

FEE(S)
☐ FEE(S) ☐ FREE

SIGHTS

WILDLIFE

POPULAR ATTRACTIONS I VISITED	
☐	☐
☐	☐
☐	☐

OVERALL EXPERIENCE

NATIONAL PARKS *Journal*

DATE(S) | VISITED

☐ SPRING ☐ SUMMER ☐ FALL ☐ WINTER

MY FAVORITE MOMENT

WHO I WENT WITH

LODING

WEATHER

FEE(S)

☐ FEE(S) ☐ FREE

SIGHTS

WILDLIFE

POPULAR ATTRACTIONS I VISITED

☐ ☐
☐ ☐
☐ ☐

OVERALL EXPERIENCE

NATIONAL PARKS *Journal*

DATE(S) | VISITED

☐ SPRING ☐ SUMMER ☐ FALL ☐ WINTER

MY FAVORITE MOMENT

WHO I WENT WITH

LODING

WEATHER

FEE(S)

☐ FEE(S) ☐ FREE

SIGHTS

WILDLIFE

POPULAR ATTRACTIONS I VISITED

☐	☐
☐	☐
☐	☐

OVERALL EXPERIENCE

NATIONAL PARKS *Journal*

DATE(S) | VISITED

☐ SPRING ☐ SUMMER ☐ FALL ☐ WINTER

MY FAVORITE MOMENT

WHO I WENT WITH

LODING

WEATHER

FEE(S)

☐ FEE(S) ☐ FREE

SIGHTS

WILDLIFE

POPULAR ATTRACTIONS I VISITED

☐ ☐

☐ ☐

☐ ☐

OVERALL EXPERIENCE

NATIONAL PARKS *Journal*

DATE(S) | VISITED

☐ SPRING ☐ SUMMER ☐ FALL ☐ WINTER

MY FAVORITE MOMENT

WHO I WENT WITH

LODING

WEATHER

FEE(S)

☐ FEE(S) ☐ FREE

SIGHTS

WILDLIFE

POPULAR ATTRACTIONS I VISITED

☐	☐
☐	☐
☐	☐

OVERALL EXPERIENCE

NATIONAL PARKS *Journal*

DATE(S) | VISITED
☐ SPRING ☐ SUMMER ☐ FALL ☐ WINTER

MY FAVORITE MOMENT

WHO I WENT WITH

LODING

WEATHER

FEE(S)
☐ FEE(S) ☐ FREE

SIGHTS

WILDLIFE

POPULAR ATTRACTIONS I VISITED	
☐	☐
☐	☐
☐	☐

OVERALL EXPERIENCE

NATIONAL PARKS *Journal*

DATE(S) | VISITED

☐ SPRING ☐ SUMMER ☐ FALL ☐ WINTER

MY FAVORITE MOMENT

WHO I WENT WITH

LODING

WEATHER

FEE(S)

☐ FEE(S) ☐ FREE

SIGHTS

WILDLIFE

POPULAR ATTRACTIONS I VISITED

☐	☐
☐	☐
☐	☐

OVERALL EXPERIENCE

NATIONAL PARKS *Journal*

DATE(S) | VISITED

☐ SPRING ☐ SUMMER ☐ FALL ☐ WINTER

MY FAVORITE MOMENT

WHO I WENT WITH

LODING

WEATHER

FEE(S)

☐ FEE(S) ☐ FREE

SIGHTS

WILDLIFE

POPULAR ATTRACTIONS I VISITED

☐ ☐
☐ ☐
☐ ☐

OVERALL EXPERIENCE

NATIONAL PARKS *Journal*

DATE(S) | VISITED

☐ SPRING ☐ SUMMER ☐ FALL ☐ WINTER

MY FAVORITE MOMENT

WHO I WENT WITH

LODING

WEATHER

FEE(S)

☐ FEE(S) ☐ FREE

SIGHTS

WILDLIFE

POPULAR ATTRACTIONS I VISITED

☐ ☐
☐ ☐
☐ ☐

OVERALL EXPERIENCE

NATIONAL PARKS Journal

DATE(S) | VISITED

☐ SPRING ☐ SUMMER ☐ FALL ☐ WINTER

MY FAVORITE MOMENT

WHO I WENT WITH

LODING

WEATHER

FEE(S)

☐ FEE(S) ☐ FREE

SIGHTS

WILDLIFE

POPULAR ATTRACTIONS I VISITED

☐ ☐

☐ ☐

☐ ☐

OVERALL EXPERIENCE

NATIONAL PARKS *Journal*

DATE(S) | VISITED

☐ SPRING ☐ SUMMER ☐ FALL ☐ WINTER

MY FAVORITE MOMENT

WHO I WENT WITH

LODING

WEATHER

FEE(S)

☐ FEE(S) ☐ FREE

SIGHTS

WILDLIFE

POPULAR ATTRACTIONS I VISITED

☐	☐
☐	☐
☐	☐

OVERALL EXPERIENCE

NATIONAL PARKS *Journal*

DATE(S) | VISITED

☐ SPRING ☐ SUMMER ☐ FALL ☐ WINTER

MY FAVORITE MOMENT

WHO I WENT WITH

LODING

WEATHER

FEE(S)

☐ FEE(S) ☐ FREE

SIGHTS

WILDLIFE

POPULAR ATTRACTIONS I VISITED

☐	☐
☐	☐
☐	☐

OVERALL EXPERIENCE

NATIONAL PARKS *Journal*

DATE(S) | VISITED

☐ SPRING ☐ SUMMER ☐ FALL ☐ WINTER

MY FAVORITE MOMENT

WHO I WENT WITH

LODING

WEATHER

FEE(S)

☐ FEE(S) ☐ FREE

SIGHTS

WILDLIFE

POPULAR ATTRACTIONS I VISITED

☐	☐
☐	☐
☐	☐

OVERALL EXPERIENCE

NATIONAL PARKS *Journal*

DATE(S) | VISITED

☐ SPRING ☐ SUMMER ☐ FALL ☐ WINTER

MY FAVORITE MOMENT

WHO I WENT WITH

LODING

WEATHER

FEE(S)

☐ FEE(S) ☐ FREE

SIGHTS

WILDLIFE

POPULAR ATTRACTIONS I VISITED

☐	☐
☐	☐
☐	☐

OVERALL EXPERIENCE

NATIONAL PARKS *Journal*

DATE(S) | VISITED

☐ SPRING ☐ SUMMER ☐ FALL ☐ WINTER

MY FAVORITE MOMENT

WHO I WENT WITH

LODING

WEATHER

FEE(S)

☐ FEE(S) ☐ FREE

SIGHTS

WILDLIFE

POPULAR ATTRACTIONS I VISITED

☐ ☐
☐ ☐
☐ ☐

OVERALL EXPERIENCE

NATIONAL PARKS *Journal*

DATE(S) | VISITED

☐ SPRING ☐ SUMMER ☐ FALL ☐ WINTER

MY FAVORITE MOMENT

WHO I WENT WITH

LODING

WEATHER

FEE(S)

☐ FEE(S) ☐ FREE

SIGHTS

WILDLIFE

POPULAR ATTRACTIONS I VISITED

☐	☐
☐	☐
☐	☐

OVERALL EXPERIENCE

NATIONAL PARKS *Journal*

DATE(S) | VISITED

☐ SPRING ☐ SUMMER ☐ FALL ☐ WINTER

MY FAVORITE MOMENT

WHO I WENT WITH

LODING

WEATHER

FEE(S)

☐ FEE(S) ☐ FREE

SIGHTS

WILDLIFE

POPULAR ATTRACTIONS I VISITED

☐	☐
☐	☐
☐	☐

OVERALL EXPERIENCE

NATIONAL PARKS *Journal*

DATE(S) | VISITED

☐ SPRING ☐ SUMMER ☐ FALL ☐ WINTER

MY FAVORITE MOMENT

WHO I WENT WITH

LODING

WEATHER

FEE(S)

☐ FEE(S) ☐ FREE

SIGHTS

WILDLIFE

POPULAR ATTRACTIONS I VISITED

☐ ☐
☐ ☐
☐ ☐

OVERALL EXPERIENCE

NATIONAL PARKS *Journal*

DATE(S) | VISITED

☐ SPRING ☐ SUMMER ☐ FALL ☐ WINTER

MY FAVORITE MOMENT

WHO I WENT WITH

LODING

WEATHER

FEE(S)

☐ FEE(S) ☐ FREE

SIGHTS

WILDLIFE

POPULAR ATTRACTIONS I VISITED

☐	☐
☐	☐
☐	☐

OVERALL EXPERIENCE

NATIONAL PARKS *Journal*

DATE(S) | VISITED

☐ SPRING ☐ SUMMER ☐ FALL ☐ WINTER

MY FAVORITE MOMENT

WHO I WENT WITH

LODING

WEATHER

FEE(S)

☐ FEE(S) ☐ FREE

SIGHTS

WILDLIFE

POPULAR ATTRACTIONS I VISITED

☐	☐
☐	☐
☐	☐

OVERALL EXPERIENCE

NATIONAL PARKS *Journal*

DATE(S) | VISITED

☐ SPRING ☐ SUMMER ☐ FALL ☐ WINTER

MY FAVORITE MOMENT

WHO I WENT WITH

LODING

WEATHER

FEE(S)

☐ FEE(S) ☐ FREE

SIGHTS

WILDLIFE

POPULAR ATTRACTIONS I VISITED

☐	☐
☐	☐
☐	☐

OVERALL EXPERIENCE

NATIONAL PARKS *Journal*

DATE(S) | VISITED

☐ SPRING ☐ SUMMER ☐ FALL ☐ WINTER

MY FAVORITE MOMENT

WHO I WENT WITH

LODING

WEATHER

FEE(S)

☐ FEE(S) ☐ FREE

SIGHTS

WILDLIFE

POPULAR ATTRACTIONS I VISITED

☐ ☐
☐ ☐
☐ ☐

OVERALL EXPERIENCE

NATIONAL PARKS *Journal*

DATE(S) | VISITED

☐ SPRING ☐ SUMMER ☐ FALL ☐ WINTER

MY FAVORITE MOMENT

WHO I WENT WITH

LODING

WEATHER

FEE(S)

☐ FEE(S) ☐ FREE

SIGHTS

WILDLIFE

POPULAR ATTRACTIONS I VISITED

☐	☐
☐	☐
☐	☐

OVERALL EXPERIENCE

NATIONAL PARKS *Journal*

DATE(S) | VISITED
☐ SPRING ☐ SUMMER ☐ FALL ☐ WINTER

MY FAVORITE MOMENT

WHO I WENT WITH

LODING

WEATHER

FEE(S)
☐ FEE(S) ☐ FREE

SIGHTS

WILDLIFE

POPULAR ATTRACTIONS I VISITED	
☐	☐
☐	☐
☐	☐

OVERALL EXPERIENCE

NATIONAL PARKS *Journal*

DATE(S) | VISITED

☐ SPRING ☐ SUMMER ☐ FALL ☐ WINTER

MY FAVORITE MOMENT

WHO I WENT WITH

LODING

WEATHER

FEE(S)

☐ FEE(S) ☐ FREE

SIGHTS

WILDLIFE

POPULAR ATTRACTIONS I VISITED

☐ ☐
☐ ☐
☐ ☐

OVERALL EXPERIENCE

NATIONAL PARKS *Journal*

DATE(S) | VISITED
☐ SPRING ☐ SUMMER ☐ FALL ☐ WINTER

WHO I WENT WITH

MY FAVORITE MOMENT

LODING

WEATHER

FEE(S)	
☐ FEE(S)	☐ FREE

SIGHTS

WILDLIFE

POPULAR ATTRACTIONS I VISITED	
☐	☐
☐	☐
☐	☐

OVERALL EXPERIENCE

NATIONAL PARKS *Journal*

DATE(S) | VISITED

☐ SPRING ☐ SUMMER ☐ FALL ☐ WINTER

MY FAVORITE MOMENT

WHO I WENT WITH

LODING

WEATHER

FEE(S)

☐ FEE(S) ☐ FREE

SIGHTS

WILDLIFE

POPULAR ATTRACTIONS I VISITED

☐ ☐
☐ ☐
☐ ☐

OVERALL EXPERIENCE

NATIONAL PARKS *Journal*

DATE(S) | VISITED
☐ SPRING ☐ SUMMER ☐ FALL ☐ WINTER

MY FAVORITE MOMENT

WHO I WENT WITH

LODING

WEATHER

FEE(S)	
☐ FEE(S)	☐ FREE

SIGHTS

WILDLIFE

POPULAR ATTRACTIONS I VISITED	
☐	☐
☐	☐
☐	☐

OVERALL EXPERIENCE

NATIONAL PARKS *Journal*

DATE(S) | VISITED

☐ SPRING ☐ SUMMER ☐ FALL ☐ WINTER

MY FAVORITE MOMENT

WHO I WENT WITH

LODING

WEATHER

FEE(S)

☐ FEE(S) ☐ FREE

SIGHTS

WILDLIFE

POPULAR ATTRACTIONS I VISITED

☐ ☐
☐ ☐
☐ ☐

OVERALL EXPERIENCE

NATIONAL PARKS *Journal*

DATE(S) | VISITED

☐ SPRING ☐ SUMMER ☐ FALL ☐ WINTER

MY FAVORITE MOMENT

WHO I WENT WITH

LODING

WEATHER

FEE(S)

☐ FEE(S) ☐ FREE

SIGHTS

WILDLIFE

POPULAR ATTRACTIONS I VISITED

☐
☐
☐
☐
☐
☐

OVERALL EXPERIENCE

NATIONAL PARKS *Journal*

DATE(S) | VISITED

☐ SPRING ☐ SUMMER ☐ FALL ☐ WINTER

MY FAVORITE MOMENT

WHO I WENT WITH

LODING

WEATHER

FEE(S)

☐ FEE(S) ☐ FREE

SIGHTS

WILDLIFE

POPULAR ATTRACTIONS I VISITED

☐	☐
☐	☐
☐	☐

OVERALL EXPERIENCE

NATIONAL PARKS *Journal*

DATE(S) | VISITED

☐ SPRING ☐ SUMMER ☐ FALL ☐ WINTER

MY FAVORITE MOMENT

WHO I WENT WITH

LODING

WEATHER

FEE(S)

☐ FEE(S) ☐ FREE

SIGHTS

WILDLIFE

POPULAR ATTRACTIONS I VISITED

☐	☐
☐	☐
☐	☐

OVERALL EXPERIENCE

NATIONAL PARKS *Journal*

DATE(S) | VISITED

☐ SPRING ☐ SUMMER ☐ FALL ☐ WINTER

MY FAVORITE MOMENT

WHO I WENT WITH

LODING

WEATHER

FEE(S)

☐ FEE(S) ☐ FREE

SIGHTS

WILDLIFE

POPULAR ATTRACTIONS I VISITED

☐ ☐
☐ ☐
☐ ☐

OVERALL EXPERIENCE

NATIONAL PARKS *Journal*

DATE(S) | VISITED

☐ SPRING ☐ SUMMER ☐ FALL ☐ WINTER

MY FAVORITE MOMENT

WHO I WENT WITH

LODING

WEATHER

FEE(S)

☐ FEE(S) ☐ FREE

SIGHTS

WILDLIFE

POPULAR ATTRACTIONS I VISITED

☐ ☐
☐ ☐
☐ ☐

OVERALL EXPERIENCE

NATIONAL PARKS *Journal*

DATE(S) | VISITED

☐ SPRING ☐ SUMMER ☐ FALL ☐ WINTER

MY FAVORITE MOMENT

WHO I WENT WITH

LODING

WEATHER

FEE(S)

☐ FEE(S) ☐ FREE

SIGHTS

WILDLIFE

POPULAR ATTRACTIONS I VISITED

☐ ☐
☐ ☐
☐ ☐

OVERALL EXPERIENCE

NATIONAL PARKS *Journal*

DATE(S) | VISITED

☐ SPRING ☐ SUMMER ☐ FALL ☐ WINTER

MY FAVORITE MOMENT

WHO I WENT WITH

LODING

WEATHER

FEE(S)

☐ FEE(S) ☐ FREE

SIGHTS

WILDLIFE

POPULAR ATTRACTIONS I VISITED

☐	☐
☐	☐
☐	☐

OVERALL EXPERIENCE

NATIONAL PARKS *Journal*

DATE(S) | VISITED

☐ SPRING ☐ SUMMER ☐ FALL ☐ WINTER

MY FAVORITE MOMENT

WHO I WENT WITH

LODING

WEATHER

FEE(S)

☐ FEE(S) ☐ FREE

SIGHTS

WILDLIFE

POPULAR ATTRACTIONS I VISITED

☐ ☐
☐ ☐
☐ ☐

OVERALL EXPERIENCE

NATIONAL PARKS *Journal*

DATE(S) | VISITED
☐ SPRING ☐ SUMMER ☐ FALL ☐ WINTER

MY FAVORITE MOMENT

WHO I WENT WITH

LODING

WEATHER

FEE(S)	
☐ FEE(S)	☐ FREE

SIGHTS

WILDLIFE

POPULAR ATTRACTIONS I VISITED	
☐	☐
☐	☐
☐	☐

OVERALL EXPERIENCE

NATIONAL PARKS *Journal*

DATE(S) | VISITED

☐ SPRING ☐ SUMMER ☐ FALL ☐ WINTER

MY FAVORITE MOMENT

WHO I WENT WITH

LODING

WEATHER

FEE(S)

☐ FEE(S) ☐ FREE

SIGHTS

WILDLIFE

POPULAR ATTRACTIONS I VISITED

☐ ☐
☐ ☐
☐ ☐

OVERALL EXPERIENCE

NATIONAL PARKS *Journal*

DATE(S) | VISITED
☐ SPRING ☐ SUMMER ☐ FALL ☐ WINTER

MY FAVORITE MOMENT

WHO I WENT WITH

LODING

WEATHER

FEE(S)	
☐ FEE(S)	☐ FREE

SIGHTS

WILDLIFE

POPULAR ATTRACTIONS I VISITED	
☐	☐
☐	☐
☐	☐

OVERALL EXPERIENCE

NATIONAL PARKS *Journal*

DATE(S) | VISITED
☐ SPRING ☐ SUMMER ☐ FALL ☐ WINTER

MY FAVORITE MOMENT

WHO I WENT WITH

LODING

WEATHER

FEE(S)
☐ FEE(S) ☐ FREE

SIGHTS

WILDLIFE

POPULAR ATTRACTIONS I VISITED	
☐	☐
☐	☐
☐	☐

OVERALL EXPERIENCE

NATIONAL PARKS *Journal*

DATE(S) | VISITED

☐ SPRING ☐ SUMMER ☐ FALL ☐ WINTER

MY FAVORITE MOMENT

WHO I WENT WITH

LODING

WEATHER

FEE(S)

☐ FEE(S) ☐ FREE

SIGHTS

WILDLIFE

POPULAR ATTRACTIONS I VISITED

☐	☐
☐	☐
☐	☐

OVERALL EXPERIENCE

NATIONAL PARKS *Journal*

DATE(S) | VISITED
☐ SPRING ☐ SUMMER ☐ FALL ☐ WINTER

WHO I WENT WITH

MY FAVORITE MOMENT

LODING

WEATHER

FEE(S)
☐ FEE(S) ☐ FREE

SIGHTS

WILDLIFE

POPULAR ATTRACTIONS I VISITED	
☐	☐
☐	☐
☐	☐

OVERALL EXPERIENCE

NATIONAL PARKS *Journal*

DATE(S) | VISITED

☐ SPRING ☐ SUMMER ☐ FALL ☐ WINTER

MY FAVORITE MOMENT

WHO I WENT WITH

LODING

WEATHER

FEE(S)

☐ FEE(S) ☐ FREE

SIGHTS

WILDLIFE

POPULAR ATTRACTIONS I VISITED

☐ ☐
☐ ☐
☐ ☐

OVERALL EXPERIENCE

NATIONAL PARKS *Journal*

DATE(S) | VISITED

☐ SPRING ☐ SUMMER ☐ FALL ☐ WINTER

MY FAVORITE MOMENT

WHO I WENT WITH

LODING

WEATHER

FEE(S)

☐ FEE(S) ☐ FREE

SIGHTS

WILDLIFE

POPULAR ATTRACTIONS I VISITED

☐ ☐
☐ ☐
☐ ☐

OVERALL EXPERIENCE

NATIONAL PARKS *Journal*

DATE(S) | VISITED
☐ SPRING ☐ SUMMER ☐ FALL ☐ WINTER

MY FAVORITE MOMENT

WHO I WENT WITH

LODING

WEATHER

FEE(S)
☐ FEE(S) ☐ FREE

SIGHTS

WILDLIFE

POPULAR ATTRACTIONS I VISITED	
☐	☐
☐	☐
☐	☐

OVERALL EXPERIENCE

NATIONAL PARKS *Journal*

DATE(S) | VISITED

☐ SPRING ☐ SUMMER ☐ FALL ☐ WINTER

MY FAVORITE MOMENT

WHO I WENT WITH

LODING

WEATHER

FEE(S)

☐ FEE(S) ☐ FREE

SIGHTS

WILDLIFE

POPULAR ATTRACTIONS I VISITED

☐ ☐
☐ ☐
☐ ☐

OVERALL EXPERIENCE

NATIONAL PARKS *Journal*

DATE(S) | VISITED

☐ SPRING ☐ SUMMER ☐ FALL ☐ WINTER

MY FAVORITE MOMENT

WHO I WENT WITH

LODING

WEATHER

FEE(S)

☐ FEE(S) ☐ FREE

SIGHTS

WILDLIFE

POPULAR ATTRACTIONS I VISITED

☐	☐
☐	☐
☐	☐

OVERALL EXPERIENCE

NATIONAL PARKS *Journal*

DATE(S) | VISITED

☐ SPRING ☐ SUMMER ☐ FALL ☐ WINTER

MY FAVORITE MOMENT

WHO I WENT WITH

LODING

WEATHER

FEE(S)

☐ FEE(S) ☐ FREE

SIGHTS

WILDLIFE

POPULAR ATTRACTIONS I VISITED

☐	☐
☐	☐
☐	☐

OVERALL EXPERIENCE

NATIONAL PARKS *Journal*

DATE(S) | VISITED

☐ SPRING ☐ SUMMER ☐ FALL ☐ WINTER

MY FAVORITE MOMENT

WHO I WENT WITH

LODING

WEATHER

FEE(S)

☐ FEE(S) ☐ FREE

SIGHTS

WILDLIFE

POPULAR ATTRACTIONS I VISITED

☐ ☐
☐ ☐
☐ ☐

OVERALL EXPERIENCE

NATIONAL PARKS *Journal*

DATE(S) | VISITED

☐ SPRING ☐ SUMMER ☐ FALL ☐ WINTER

MY FAVORITE MOMENT

WHO I WENT WITH

LODING

WEATHER

FEE(S)

☐ FEE(S) ☐ FREE

SIGHTS

WILDLIFE

POPULAR ATTRACTIONS I VISITED

☐ ☐
☐ ☐
☐ ☐

OVERALL EXPERIENCE

NATIONAL PARKS *Journal*

DATE(S) | VISITED

☐ SPRING ☐ SUMMER ☐ FALL ☐ WINTER

MY FAVORITE MOMENT

WHO I WENT WITH

LODING

WEATHER

FEE(S)

☐ FEE(S) ☐ FREE

SIGHTS

WILDLIFE

POPULAR ATTRACTIONS I VISITED

☐ ☐
☐ ☐
☐ ☐

OVERALL EXPERIENCE

NATIONAL PARKS *Journal*

DATE(S) | VISITED

☐ SPRING ☐ SUMMER ☐ FALL ☐ WINTER

MY FAVORITE MOMENT

WHO I WENT WITH

LODING

WEATHER

FEE(S)

☐ FEE(S) ☐ FREE

SIGHTS

WILDLIFE

POPULAR ATTRACTIONS I VISITED

☐ ☐
☐ ☐
☐ ☐

OVERALL EXPERIENCE

NATIONAL PARKS *Journal*

DATE(S) | VISITED
☐ SPRING ☐ SUMMER ☐ FALL ☐ WINTER

MY FAVORITE MOMENT

WHO I WENT WITH

LODING

WEATHER

FEE(S)	
☐ FEE(S)	☐ FREE

SIGHTS

WILDLIFE

POPULAR ATTRACTIONS I VISITED	
☐	☐
☐	☐
☐	☐

OVERALL EXPERIENCE

NATIONAL PARKS *Journal*

DATE(S) | VISITED

☐ SPRING ☐ SUMMER ☐ FALL ☐ WINTER

MY FAVORITE MOMENT

WHO I WENT WITH

LODING

WEATHER

FEE(S)

☐ FEE(S) ☐ FREE

SIGHTS

WILDLIFE

POPULAR ATTRACTIONS I VISITED

☐ ☐
☐ ☐
☐ ☐

OVERALL EXPERIENCE

NATIONAL PARKS *Journal*

DATE(S) | VISITED
☐ SPRING ☐ SUMMER ☐ FALL ☐ WINTER

WHO I WENT WITH

MY FAVORITE MOMENT

LODING

WEATHER

FEE(S)
☐ FEE(S) ☐ FREE

SIGHTS

WILDLIFE

POPULAR ATTRACTIONS I VISITED	
☐	☐
☐	☐
☐	☐

OVERALL EXPERIENCE

NATIONAL PARKS *Journal*

DATE(S) | VISITED

☐ SPRING ☐ SUMMER ☐ FALL ☐ WINTER

MY FAVORITE MOMENT

WHO I WENT WITH

LODING

WEATHER

FEE(S)

☐ FEE(S) ☐ FREE

SIGHTS

WILDLIFE

POPULAR ATTRACTIONS I VISITED

☐	☐
☐	☐
☐	☐

OVERALL EXPERIENCE

NATIONAL PARKS *Journal*

DATE(S) | VISITED
☐ SPRING ☐ SUMMER ☐ FALL ☐ WINTER

MY FAVORITE MOMENT

WHO I WENT WITH

LODING

WEATHER

FEE(S)
☐ FEE(S) ☐ FREE

SIGHTS

WILDLIFE

POPULAR ATTRACTIONS I VISITED	
☐	☐
☐	☐
☐	☐

OVERALL EXPERIENCE

NATIONAL PARKS *Journal*

DATE(S) | VISITED

☐ SPRING ☐ SUMMER ☐ FALL ☐ WINTER

MY FAVORITE MOMENT

WHO I WENT WITH

LODING

WEATHER

FEE(S)

☐ FEE(S) ☐ FREE

SIGHTS

WILDLIFE

POPULAR ATTRACTIONS I VISITED

☐	☐
☐	☐
☐	☐

OVERALL EXPERIENCE

NATIONAL PARKS *Journal*

DATE(S) | VISITED

☐ SPRING ☐ SUMMER ☐ FALL ☐ WINTER

MY FAVORITE MOMENT

WHO I WENT WITH

LODING

WEATHER

FEE(S)

☐ FEE(S) ☐ FREE

SIGHTS

WILDLIFE

POPULAR ATTRACTIONS I VISITED

☐	☐
☐	☐
☐	☐

OVERALL EXPERIENCE

NATIONAL PARKS *Journal*

DATE(S) | VISITED

☐ SPRING ☐ SUMMER ☐ FALL ☐ WINTER

MY FAVORITE MOMENT

WHO I WENT WITH

LODING

WEATHER

FEE(S)

☐ FEE(S) ☐ FREE

SIGHTS

WILDLIFE

POPULAR ATTRACTIONS I VISITED

☐	☐
☐	☐
☐	☐

OVERALL EXPERIENCE

NATIONAL PARKS *Journal*

DATE(S) | VISITED

☐ SPRING ☐ SUMMER ☐ FALL ☐ WINTER

MY FAVORITE MOMENT

WHO I WENT WITH

LODING

WEATHER

FEE(S)

☐ FEE(S) ☐ FREE

SIGHTS

WILDLIFE

POPULAR ATTRACTIONS I VISITED

☐ ☐
☐ ☐
☐ ☐

OVERALL EXPERIENCE

NATIONAL PARKS *Journal*

DATE(S) | VISITED

☐ SPRING ☐ SUMMER ☐ FALL ☐ WINTER

MY FAVORITE MOMENT

WHO I WENT WITH

LODING

WEATHER

FEE(S)

☐ FEE(S) ☐ FREE

SIGHTS

WILDLIFE

POPULAR ATTRACTIONS I VISITED

☐	☐
☐	☐
☐	☐

OVERALL EXPERIENCE

NATIONAL PARKS *Journal*

DATE(S) | VISITED

☐ SPRING ☐ SUMMER ☐ FALL ☐ WINTER

MY FAVORITE MOMENT

WHO I WENT WITH

LODING

WEATHER

FEE(S)

☐ FEE(S) ☐ FREE

SIGHTS

WILDLIFE

POPULAR ATTRACTIONS I VISITED

☐	☐
☐	☐
☐	☐

OVERALL EXPERIENCE

NATIONAL PARKS *Journal*

DATE(S) | VISITED

☐ SPRING ☐ SUMMER ☐ FALL ☐ WINTER

MY FAVORITE MOMENT

WHO I WENT WITH

LODING

WEATHER

FEE(S)

☐ FEE(S) ☐ FREE

SIGHTS

WILDLIFE

POPULAR ATTRACTIONS I VISITED

☐	☐
☐	☐
☐	☐

OVERALL EXPERIENCE

NATIONAL PARKS *Journal*

DATE(S) | VISITED

☐ SPRING ☐ SUMMER ☐ FALL ☐ WINTER

MY FAVORITE MOMENT

WHO I WENT WITH

LODING

WEATHER

FEE(S)

☐ FEE(S) ☐ FREE

SIGHTS

WILDLIFE

POPULAR ATTRACTIONS I VISITED

☐	☐
☐	☐
☐	☐

OVERALL EXPERIENCE

NATIONAL PARKS *Journal*

DATE(S) | VISITED

☐ SPRING ☐ SUMMER ☐ FALL ☐ WINTER

MY FAVORITE MOMENT

WHO I WENT WITH

LODING

WEATHER

FEE(S)

☐ FEE(S) ☐ FREE

SIGHTS

WILDLIFE

POPULAR ATTRACTIONS I VISITED

☐	☐
☐	☐
☐	☐

OVERALL EXPERIENCE

NATIONAL PARKS *Journal*

DATE(S) | VISITED

☐ SPRING ☐ SUMMER ☐ FALL ☐ WINTER

MY FAVORITE MOMENT

WHO I WENT WITH

LODING

WEATHER

FEE(S)

☐ FEE(S) ☐ FREE

SIGHTS

WILDLIFE

POPULAR ATTRACTIONS I VISITED

☐	☐
☐	☐
☐	☐

OVERALL EXPERIENCE

NATIONAL PARKS *Journal*

DATE(S) | VISITED

☐ SPRING ☐ SUMMER ☐ FALL ☐ WINTER

MY FAVORITE MOMENT

WHO I WENT WITH

LODING

WEATHER

FEE(S)

☐ FEE(S) ☐ FREE

SIGHTS

WILDLIFE

POPULAR ATTRACTIONS I VISITED

☐ ☐
☐ ☐
☐ ☐

OVERALL EXPERIENCE

NATIONAL PARKS *Journal*

DATE(S) | VISITED
☐ SPRING ☐ SUMMER ☐ FALL ☐ WINTER

MY FAVORITE MOMENT

WHO I WENT WITH

LODING

WEATHER

FEE(S)
☐ FEE(S) ☐ FREE

SIGHTS

WILDLIFE

POPULAR ATTRACTIONS I VISITED	
☐	☐
☐	☐
☐	☐

OVERALL EXPERIENCE

NATIONAL PARKS *Journal*

DATE(S) | VISITED

☐ SPRING ☐ SUMMER ☐ FALL ☐ WINTER

MY FAVORITE MOMENT

WHO I WENT WITH

LODING

WEATHER

FEE(S)

☐ FEE(S) ☐ FREE

SIGHTS

WILDLIFE

POPULAR ATTRACTIONS I VISITED

☐ ☐
☐ ☐
☐ ☐

OVERALL EXPERIENCE

NATIONAL PARKS *Journal*

DATE(S) | VISITED

☐ SPRING ☐ SUMMER ☐ FALL ☐ WINTER

MY FAVORITE MOMENT

WHO I WENT WITH

LODING

WEATHER

FEE(S)

☐ FEE(S) ☐ FREE

SIGHTS

WILDLIFE

POPULAR ATTRACTIONS I VISITED

☐	☐
☐	☐
☐	☐

OVERALL EXPERIENCE

NATIONAL PARKS *Journal*

DATE(S) | VISITED
☐ SPRING ☐ SUMMER ☐ FALL ☐ WINTER

MY FAVORITE MOMENT

WHO I WENT WITH

LODING

WEATHER

FEE(S)
☐ FEE(S) ☐ FREE

SIGHTS

WILDLIFE

POPULAR ATTRACTIONS I VISITED	
☐	☐
☐	☐
☐	☐

OVERALL EXPERIENCE

NATIONAL PARKS *Journal*

DATE(S) | VISITED

☐ SPRING ☐ SUMMER ☐ FALL ☐ WINTER

MY FAVORITE MOMENT

WHO I WENT WITH

LODING

WEATHER

FEE(S)

☐ FEE(S) ☐ FREE

SIGHTS

WILDLIFE

POPULAR ATTRACTIONS I VISITED

☐	☐
☐	☐
☐	☐

OVERALL EXPERIENCE

NATIONAL PARKS *Journal*

DATE(S) | VISITED

☐ SPRING ☐ SUMMER ☐ FALL ☐ WINTER

MY FAVORITE MOMENT

WHO I WENT WITH

LODING

WEATHER

FEE(S)

☐ FEE(S) ☐ FREE

SIGHTS

WILDLIFE

POPULAR ATTRACTIONS I VISITED

☐	☐
☐	☐
☐	☐

OVERALL EXPERIENCE

NATIONAL PARKS *Journal*

DATE(S) | VISITED

☐ SPRING ☐ SUMMER ☐ FALL ☐ WINTER

MY FAVORITE MOMENT

WHO I WENT WITH

LODING

WEATHER

FEE(S)

☐ FEE(S) ☐ FREE

SIGHTS

WILDLIFE

POPULAR ATTRACTIONS I VISITED

☐	☐
☐	☐
☐	☐

OVERALL EXPERIENCE

NATIONAL PARKS *Journal*

DATE(S) | VISITED
☐ SPRING ☐ SUMMER ☐ FALL ☐ WINTER

MY FAVORITE MOMENT

WHO I WENT WITH

LODING

WEATHER

FEE(S)	
☐ FEE(S)	☐ FREE

SIGHTS

WILDLIFE

POPULAR ATTRACTIONS I VISITED	
☐	☐
☐	☐
☐	☐

OVERALL EXPERIENCE

NATIONAL PARKS *Journal*

DATE(S) | VISITED

☐ SPRING ☐ SUMMER ☐ FALL ☐ WINTER

MY FAVORITE MOMENT

WHO I WENT WITH

LODING

WEATHER

FEE(S)

☐ FEE(S) ☐ FREE

SIGHTS

WILDLIFE

POPULAR ATTRACTIONS I VISITED

☐ ☐
☐ ☐
☐ ☐

OVERALL EXPERIENCE

NATIONAL PARKS *Journal*

DATE(S) | VISITED

☐ SPRING ☐ SUMMER ☐ FALL ☐ WINTER

MY FAVORITE MOMENT

WHO I WENT WITH

LODING

WEATHER

FEE(S)

☐ FEE(S) ☐ FREE

SIGHTS

WILDLIFE

POPULAR ATTRACTIONS I VISITED

☐	☐
☐	☐
☐	☐

OVERALL EXPERIENCE

NATIONAL PARKS *Journal*

DATE(S) | VISITED
☐ SPRING ☐ SUMMER ☐ FALL ☐ WINTER

MY FAVORITE MOMENT

WHO I WENT WITH

LODING

WEATHER

FEE(S)
☐ FEE(S) ☐ FREE

SIGHTS

WILDLIFE

POPULAR ATTRACTIONS I VISITED	
☐	☐
☐	☐
☐	☐

OVERALL EXPERIENCE

NATIONAL PARKS *Journal*

DATE(S) | VISITED

☐ SPRING ☐ SUMMER ☐ FALL ☐ WINTER

MY FAVORITE MOMENT

WHO I WENT WITH

LODING

WEATHER

FEE(S)

☐ FEE(S) ☐ FREE

SIGHTS

WILDLIFE

POPULAR ATTRACTIONS I VISITED

☐ ☐

☐ ☐

☐ ☐

OVERALL EXPERIENCE

NATIONAL PARKS *Journal*

DATE(S) | VISITED

☐ SPRING ☐ SUMMER ☐ FALL ☐ WINTER

MY FAVORITE MOMENT

WHO I WENT WITH

LODING

WEATHER

FEE(S)

☐ FEE(S) ☐ FREE

SIGHTS

WILDLIFE

POPULAR ATTRACTIONS I VISITED

☐ ☐
☐ ☐
☐ ☐

OVERALL EXPERIENCE

NATIONAL PARKS *Journal*

DATE(S) | VISITED

☐ SPRING ☐ SUMMER ☐ FALL ☐ WINTER

MY FAVORITE MOMENT

WHO I WENT WITH

LODING

WEATHER

FEE(S)

☐ FEE(S) ☐ FREE

SIGHTS

WILDLIFE

POPULAR ATTRACTIONS I VISITED

☐	☐
☐	☐
☐	☐

OVERALL EXPERIENCE

NATIONAL PARKS *Journal*

DATE(S) | VISITED

☐ SPRING ☐ SUMMER ☐ FALL ☐ WINTER

MY FAVORITE MOMENT

WHO I WENT WITH

LODING

WEATHER

FEE(S)

☐ FEE(S) ☐ FREE

SIGHTS

WILDLIFE

POPULAR ATTRACTIONS I VISITED

☐	☐
☐	☐
☐	☐

OVERALL EXPERIENCE

NATIONAL PARKS *Journal*

DATE(S) | VISITED

☐ SPRING ☐ SUMMER ☐ FALL ☐ WINTER

MY FAVORITE MOMENT

WHO I WENT WITH

LODING

WEATHER

FEE(S)

☐ FEE(S) ☐ FREE

SIGHTS

WILDLIFE

POPULAR ATTRACTIONS I VISITED

☐	☐
☐	☐
☐	☐

OVERALL EXPERIENCE

NATIONAL PARKS *Journal*

DATE(S) | VISITED

☐ SPRING ☐ SUMMER ☐ FALL ☐ WINTER

MY FAVORITE MOMENT

WHO I WENT WITH

LODING

WEATHER

FEE(S)

☐ FEE(S) ☐ FREE

SIGHTS

WILDLIFE

POPULAR ATTRACTIONS I VISITED

☐ ☐
☐ ☐
☐ ☐

OVERALL EXPERIENCE

NATIONAL PARKS *Journal*

DATE(S) | VISITED

☐ SPRING ☐ SUMMER ☐ FALL ☐ WINTER

MY FAVORITE MOMENT

WHO I WENT WITH

LODING

WEATHER

FEE(S)

☐ FEE(S) ☐ FREE

SIGHTS

WILDLIFE

POPULAR ATTRACTIONS I VISITED

☐	☐
☐	☐
☐	☐

OVERALL EXPERIENCE

NATIONAL PARKS *Journal*

DATE(S) | VISITED

☐ SPRING ☐ SUMMER ☐ FALL ☐ WINTER

MY FAVORITE MOMENT

WHO I WENT WITH

LODING

WEATHER

FEE(S)

☐ FEE(S) ☐ FREE

SIGHTS

WILDLIFE

POPULAR ATTRACTIONS I VISITED

☐	☐
☐	☐
☐	☐

OVERALL EXPERIENCE

NATIONAL PARKS *Journal*

DATE(S) | VISITED

☐ SPRING ☐ SUMMER ☐ FALL ☐ WINTER

MY FAVORITE MOMENT

WHO I WENT WITH

LODING

WEATHER

FEE(S)

☐ FEE(S) ☐ FREE

SIGHTS

WILDLIFE

POPULAR ATTRACTIONS I VISITED

☐ ☐
☐ ☐
☐ ☐

OVERALL EXPERIENCE

NATIONAL PARKS *Journal*

DATE(S) | VISITED

☐ SPRING ☐ SUMMER ☐ FALL ☐ WINTER

MY FAVORITE MOMENT

WHO I WENT WITH

LODING

WEATHER

FEE(S)

☐ FEE(S) ☐ FREE

SIGHTS

WILDLIFE

POPULAR ATTRACTIONS I VISITED

☐	☐
☐	☐
☐	☐

OVERALL EXPERIENCE

NATIONAL PARKS *Journal*

DATE(S) | VISITED

☐ SPRING ☐ SUMMER ☐ FALL ☐ WINTER

MY FAVORITE MOMENT

WHO I WENT WITH

LODING

WEATHER

FEE(S)

☐ FEE(S) ☐ FREE

SIGHTS

WILDLIFE

POPULAR ATTRACTIONS I VISITED

☐	☐
☐	☐
☐	☐

OVERALL EXPERIENCE

NATIONAL PARKS *Journal*

DATE(S) | VISITED

☐ SPRING ☐ SUMMER ☐ FALL ☐ WINTER

MY FAVORITE MOMENT

WHO I WENT WITH

LODING

WEATHER

FEE(S)

☐ FEE(S) ☐ FREE

SIGHTS

WILDLIFE

POPULAR ATTRACTIONS I VISITED

☐ ☐
☐ ☐
☐ ☐

OVERALL EXPERIENCE

NATIONAL PARKS *Journal*

DATE(S) | VISITED

☐ SPRING ☐ SUMMER ☐ FALL ☐ WINTER

MY FAVORITE MOMENT

WHO I WENT WITH

LODING

WEATHER

FEE(S)

☐ FEE(S) ☐ FREE

SIGHTS

WILDLIFE

POPULAR ATTRACTIONS I VISITED

☐	☐
☐	☐
☐	☐

OVERALL EXPERIENCE

NATIONAL PARKS *Journal*

DATE(S) | VISITED

☐ SPRING ☐ SUMMER ☐ FALL ☐ WINTER

MY FAVORITE MOMENT

WHO I WENT WITH

LODING

WEATHER

FEE(S)

☐ FEE(S) ☐ FREE

SIGHTS

WILDLIFE

POPULAR ATTRACTIONS I VISITED

☐ ☐
☐ ☐
☐ ☐

OVERALL EXPERIENCE

NATIONAL PARKS *Journal*

DATE(S) | VISITED

☐ SPRING ☐ SUMMER ☐ FALL ☐ WINTER

MY FAVORITE MOMENT

WHO I WENT WITH

LODING

WEATHER

FEE(S)

☐ FEE(S) ☐ FREE

SIGHTS

WILDLIFE

POPULAR ATTRACTIONS I VISITED

☐ ☐
☐ ☐
☐ ☐

OVERALL EXPERIENCE

NATIONAL PARKS *Journal*

DATE(S) | VISITED

☐ SPRING ☐ SUMMER ☐ FALL ☐ WINTER

MY FAVORITE MOMENT

WHO I WENT WITH

LODING

WEATHER

FEE(S)

☐ FEE(S) ☐ FREE

SIGHTS

WILDLIFE

POPULAR ATTRACTIONS I VISITED

☐	☐
☐	☐
☐	☐

OVERALL EXPERIENCE

NATIONAL PARKS *Journal*

DATE(S) | VISITED
☐ SPRING ☐ SUMMER ☐ FALL ☐ WINTER

MY FAVORITE MOMENT

WHO I WENT WITH

LODING

WEATHER

FEE(S)
☐ FEE(S) ☐ FREE

SIGHTS

WILDLIFE

POPULAR ATTRACTIONS I VISITED	
☐	☐
☐	☐
☐	☐

OVERALL EXPERIENCE

NATIONAL PARKS *Journal*

DATE(S) | VISITED
☐ SPRING ☐ SUMMER ☐ FALL ☐ WINTER

MY FAVORITE MOMENT

WHO I WENT WITH

LODING

WEATHER

FEE(S)	
☐ FEE(S)	☐ FREE

SIGHTS

WILDLIFE

POPULAR ATTRACTIONS I VISITED	
☐	☐
☐	☐
☐	☐

OVERALL EXPERIENCE

NATIONAL PARKS *Journal*

DATE(S) | VISITED

☐ SPRING ☐ SUMMER ☐ FALL ☐ WINTER

MY FAVORITE MOMENT

WHO I WENT WITH

LODING

WEATHER

FEE(S)

☐ FEE(S) ☐ FREE

SIGHTS

WILDLIFE

POPULAR ATTRACTIONS I VISITED

☐	☐
☐	☐
☐	☐

OVERALL EXPERIENCE

NATIONAL PARKS *Journal*

DATE(S) | VISITED

☐ SPRING ☐ SUMMER ☐ FALL ☐ WINTER

MY FAVORITE MOMENT

WHO I WENT WITH

LODING

WEATHER

FEE(S)

☐ FEE(S) ☐ FREE

SIGHTS

WILDLIFE

POPULAR ATTRACTIONS I VISITED

☐ ☐
☐ ☐
☐ ☐

OVERALL EXPERIENCE

Made in the USA
Coppell, TX
30 January 2022